External Research Associates Program

ENABLING UNITY OF EFFORT
IN HOMELAND RESPONSE OPERATIONS

H Steven Blum
Kerry McIntyre

April 2012

The views expressed in this report are those of the authors and do not necessarily reflect the official policy or position of the Department of the Army, the Department of Defense, or the U.S. Government. Authors of Strategic Studies Institute (SSI) publications enjoy full academic freedom, provided they do not disclose classified information, jeopardize operations security, or misrepresent official U.S. policy. Such academic freedom empowers them to offer new and sometimes controversial perspectives in the interest of furthering debate on key issues. This report is cleared for public release; distribution is unlimited.

*****

*****

Comments pertaining to this report are invited and should be forwarded to: Director, Strategic Studies Institute, U.S. Army War College, 45 Ashburn Dr., Bldg. 47, Carlisle, PA 17013.

*****

This manuscript was funded by the U.S. Army War College External Research Associates Program. Information on this program is available on our website, *www.StrategicStudiesInstitute. army.mil*, at the Opportunities tab.

*****

*****

The Strategic Studies Institute publishes a monthly e-mail newsletter to update the national security community on the research of our analysts, recent and forthcoming publications, and upcoming conferences sponsored by the Institute. Each newsletter also provides a strategic commentary by one of our research analysts. If you are interested in receiving this newsletter, please subscribe on the SSI website at *www.StrategicStudiesInstitute. army.mil/newsletter/*.

FOREWORD

Any significant homeland response event requires Americans to work together. This has proven to be a complex challenge. Our response capabilities, while substantial, are spread across thousands of stakeholders: federal, state, and local government agencies and organizations, nongovernmental organizations, and private industry. No single actor has all the necessary tools to respond completely to a major crisis. Despite considerable national effort and resources devoted to planning, training, integrating, and improving our homeland response capabilities, effectiveness in working together — unity of effort — still seems to elude us. Achieving unity of effort is difficult even in simple situations. It becomes increasingly complicated when it involves dozens or even hundreds of participants in a federal system such as ours, where responsibility and capability are distributed across many levels and functions. Finding ways to synergize a broad range of responsible participants is the central challenge to effective homeland response operations.

In this monograph, H Steven Blum and Kerry McIntyre argue that the problem of achieving unity of effort in homeland response is not one of poor planning or inadequate resources, but rather more fundamental. It involves the way in which thousands of participants from dissimilar professional cultures think about their roles and responsibilities for homeland response. To address this problem, Blum and McIntyre propose a broadly construed national doctrine, developed in a dynamic and responsive doctrine-producing system. They cite the example of joint military doctrine, which attained its contemporary robust state and authoritative impact only through changes implemented as a result of the Goldwater-Nichols Act. The joint doctrine-producing system that arose from Goldwater-Nichols remedied many shortcomings, such as enforcing congruity between individual service and joint doctrine, identifying and addressing capability gaps, and incorporating the requirements of field commanders. The authors contend that a dynamic national homeland response doctrine, developed in a truly inclusive national system, would have a similar effect in synergizing national capabilities. They propose a doctrinal system that develops and implements operational concepts, plans, and training programs. The concepts are thoroughly tested in realistic exercises and actual operations. The plans, operations, and training programs are then systematically analyzed to inform and update evolving doctrinal concepts, which ultimately influence the organization, training, and equipping of response elements.

Blum and McIntyre contend that such a national doctrine requires a new management concept, fashioned on the model of the military's Joint Interagency Task Force (JIATF). They argue that this concept has broad potential not just in support of military operations, but any time disparate response organizations must work together. They suggest a JIATF-like interagency coordination and action group which could operate across and between jurisdictional divides to unify not just the federal interagency response, but state and perhaps local interagency efforts as well. In developing this idea, they outline some of the critical functions this element should perform.

Finally, the authors address the problem of ensuring that our military's available "dual capable" forces—active and reserve—are contributing to unity of effort in homeland response. They discuss the nascent potential of dual-status command, the artificial impediment posed by the division of forces into separate legal statuses under Title 10 and Title 32, and the possibility of a civil support force generation model to improve predictability in providing available capabilities for homeland response.

DOUGLAS C. LOVELACE, JR.
Director
Strategic Studies Institute

ABOUT THE AUTHORS

H STEVEN BLUM served over 42 years in uniform, capping a career as the first National Guardsman to serve as a Deputy Combatant Commander. As Deputy Commander, U.S. Northern Command, he fundamentally reshaped how Americans and the U.S. military think about, prepare for, and conduct operations for homeland defense, homeland security, and defense support of civil authority. In two terms as Chief, National Guard Bureau, he transformed the National Guard from a Cold War strategic reserve into a 21st century operational force capable of joint and expeditionary warfare and flexible response to a broad range of civil and humanitarian contingencies. He was responsible for deploying over 50,000 National Guardsmen in response to Hurricane Katrina, the largest military response to a natural disaster in U.S. history. Lieutenant General (Ret.) Blum has commanded a Special Forces Detachment, an Infantry Battalion, and two brigades. As Commanding General, 29th Infantry Division, he deployed over 6,500 citizen-soldiers from 21 states to Bosnia-Herzegovina. He simultaneously served as Commanding General-Multinational Division (North) in Operation JOINT FORGE, leading a Russian airborne brigade, a Turkish Army brigade, and a Multinational Nordic-Polish brigade. General Blum currently serves as Executive-in-Residence at the Johns Hopkins University School of Education, Division of Public Safety and Leadership. He is also Managing Director and Practice Lead for Sitrick & Company, a broadly known crisis communications organization. General Blum is a frequent consultant for private and government organizations on planning, training, and disaster response.

KERRY MCINTYRE currently serves as a Strategic Planner in support of the Maryland Army National Guard. He served nearly 24 years in uniform, including more than 21 years of fulltime service in the Maryland Army National Guard. His military career includes assignments in personnel, operations, and staff management at battalion, brigade, and state (Joint Force Headquarters) level. As the Executive Officer, 58th Troop Command, he supervised daily planning and preparations for the state's ground Joint Task Force for civil support. His career includes a variety of roles in civil support operations and exercises. Lieutenant Colonel (Ret.) McIntyre is a graduate of the American University School of International Service and the U.S. Army War College.

SUMMARY

Balancing authorities and responsibilities within our federal system has been a matter of continuous debate since the earliest days of the republic. Its continued relevance is exemplified in our current national conversation over how to most effectively organize and operate for homeland security and defense. Crises and catastrophic events in our homeland require Americans from different organizations, jurisdictions, and functions to work together. Yet despite considerable national effort and resources devoted to developing and improving our collective response capabilities, effectiveness in working together — unity of effort — still seems to elude us.

Achieving unity of effort is the central challenge to effective homeland response operations. No single organization, function, or stakeholder has all the necessary tools to respond completely to the wide range of crises that routinely occur, or could occur, in our homeland. Combining the assets, capabilities, expertise, and resources of multiple participants has proven to be exceedingly complex and difficult. Our homeland response capabilities are considerable, but they are dispersed across a patchwork of jurisdictions and functions. The challenge in homeland response operations is neither inadequate resources nor lack of capabilities, but rather in being able to bring them to bear at the right time and place, and in the right combination. Disasters in our homeland have enormous consequences. Regardless of cause or extent, they always hold the potential for significant loss of life, human suffering, economic dislocation, and erosion of public confidence in government. Given all that is at stake, we must do better. There are certainly a number of ways to improve our results; this monograph proposes three specific ways to do so.

First, enhancing our capacity for unity of effort requires more than simply devoting more resources and rhetoric to the problem. The challenge is more fundamental; it requires us to change the way we think about homeland response in order to establish the intellectual pre-conditions for unified effort. Creating this cultural shift requires a national homeland response *doctrine*, formulated in a dynamic and responsive *doctrinal system*. Doctrine performs a vital unifying function in complex operations. It delineates best practices, establishes standards, and clarifies terminology, responsibilities, and procedures. It creates common understandings, bridging organizational and jurisdictional divides.

A nascent federal homeland response doctrine currently exists, codified in the National Response Framework (NRF), National Incident Management System (NIMS), and Incident Command System (ICS). Yet, a doctrinal system is larger than the doctrine itself. It operates in a dynamic cycle, providing a process to identify capability gaps, develop new operating concepts, and validate them against rigorous standards. An effective doctrinal system also incorporates all relevant stakeholders in the full cycle of concept development, validation, and integration into plans and procedures. Current homeland response doctrine is a federal, not national doctrine. A unifying national doctrine, engendered in a dynamic and responsive system, would provide the basis for developing a national culture of communication and cooperation in homeland response operations.

A second way to enhance our capacity for unity of effort is to ensure that national doctrine can be broadly implemented. A truly national homeland response doctrine system will function in an interagency, intergovernmental, multi-jurisdictional environment. Implementing it requires a new management structure that can also operate in the spaces between agencies and governments. The example of the military's Joint Interagency Task Force (JIATF) points the way toward this new structure. A permanent interagency coordination and action group, which integrates inputs, resources, and capabilities of all stakeholders, can synergize and coordinate the efforts of all. Such a structure clearly has an application at federal, state, and perhaps even local level, as each has a complex interagency framework to manage in order to fully integrate response capabilities. To be effective, this structure cannot be subordinate to any single agency or function; it must be responsive to all stakeholders and accountable to an elected leader with authority over the interagency effort.

A third way to enhance unity of effort is to remove barriers to employment of military capabilities for homeland response operations. There are clear legal restrictions on the roles and uses of our military at home, which exist for sound reasons. Yet much of our military can be characterized as "dual capable," describing forces with inherent capabilities useful both for warfighting and for civil support tasks. It makes little difference to the injured, hungry, and dispossessed that the soldier who rescued them is a National Guardsman, a Title 10 reservist, or an active duty service member. Their reasonable expectation is that the forces raised and sustained with their tax dollars will provide for their safety when needed. For this reason, we should be removing impediments to utilizing our military forces — particularly our reserve components—for homeland response operations when they are not engaged in other federal missions. This is not a matter of apportioning different forces to the National Guard. Rather, it is one of determining when and how any relevant military capabilities should be placed under a governor's authority for civil support roles. The recent development of the concept of dual status command is a step forward in this regard. Development of a predictable civil support force generation model, similar to the one employed by the services for federal missions overseas, will further enhance unity of effort by facilitating planning among the states for temporary use of dual status military capabilities.

Achieving unity of effort in homeland response is a complex challenge, among the greatest of our age. It is the single most important factor in our ability to plan for and respond effectively to disasters at home. We devote enormous resources to public safety and security at many levels. Our citizens surely have a right to expect that these resources will be well used by their leaders, elected and appointed. This means that we must find better ways to work together. It requires leaders and organizations at all levels to combine their efforts, resources, and capabilities to achieve complete and responsive solutions. It requires us to develop new ways of thinking about and managing homeland response capabilities, before disaster strikes.

ENABLING UNITY OF EFFORT
IN HOMELAND RESPONSE OPERATIONS

> Who is likely to make suitable provisions for the pub-
> lic defense, as that body to which the guardianship of
> the public safety is confided . . . which, by the exten-
> sion of its authority throughout the States, can alone
> establish uniformity and concert in the plans and mea-
> sures by which the common safety is to be secured?
>
> — Alexander Hamilton,
> *Federalist Paper No. 23*

Questions about achieving unity of effort in our public policy, and the balance of authority and responsibility between various levels of government, are as old as the republic. They have enormous contemporary relevance, particularly in the national debate over how we organize and act to secure the safety of our citizens and interests at home. We believe that achieving unity of effort is the central challenge to effective homeland response operations. Despite all the effort and considerable resources devoted to improving our capabilities, effectiveness in working together — unity of effort — still seems to elude us. In many disaster situations, including the largest and most dangerous, the ability to field a seamless, unified, robust response from our enormously capable mix of local, state, and federal government and private sector entities is still out of reach. This monograph examines how we might change our current organization and doctrine today to achieve a more effective response. For simplicity, the term "homeland response" is used to encompass all facets of planning, preparing, and resourcing for; directly responding to; and mitigating and recovering from, the broad spectrum of catastrophic events in the American homeland, ranging from natural to man-made disasters, industrial accidents, pandemic disease, terrorist attacks, and similar events.

Why Unity of Effort?

Any significant homeland response event requires Americans to work together. Doing so can be a complex challenge. Our nation has enormous resources and vast capacity available to it, but these are spread across a patchwork of jurisdictions, agencies, and authorities. No single organization, function, or stakeholder has all the necessary tools to respond completely to a major crisis, let alone many smaller ones. Combining the assets, capabilities, expertise, organizations, and resources of multiple participants is extremely difficult. This should be unsurprising; achieving unity of effort is difficult even for structurally similar, well-resourced entities operating under unified command—such as our military. It becomes increasingly complicated when it involves dozens or even hundreds of participants in a federal system such as ours, where responsibility and capability are distributed across many levels and functions. At each level of government, homeland response must combine planners and responders with diverse organizational cultures operating under separate authorities and differing, even divergent, operational requirements and objectives.

In normal times, the distribution and balancing of power in our federal system are a considerable strength, a crucial element in the vitality and responsiveness of our democracy. However, the multitude of threats we face in our homeland are not confined to the capabilities of a single function, nor within the bounds of geography or jurisdiction; both prepared-ness and response are complicated by the "seams" in our system. In his seminal work *On War*, Carl Von Clausewitz wrote that in war even the simplest things are difficult, and that "difficulties accumulate . . . pro-ducing a kind of friction." This friction is an impedi-ment that "makes the apparently easy so difficult."[1] Just as in warfare, a kind of Clausewitzian friction is quite obviously at work in every homeland response situation, in every crisis which demands collective action. The diffusion of authorities and capabilities across multiple agencies, organizations, and levels of government, coupled with the sheer size and complex-ity of the nation, creates an unavoidable friction that makes the simplest operations difficult and achieving unity of effort a daunting challenge.

Solving any problem must begin with defining it. Our homeland response problem is not one of insuffi-cient resources. We spend billions, possibly more than any other nation, on homeland response. It is not one of individual assets. We have highly developed medi-cal, police, fire, transportation, logistics, communica-tions, military, and other emergency response capabil-ities. The problem at its heart is not lacking resources and capabilities, but in being unable to bring them to bear at the right time and place, and in the right com-bination, to achieve effective results. It is the inability to integrate a vast array of systems and elements into a seamless, coordinated response. Combining what each stakeholder brings to the table requires coopera-tion, communication, collaboration, and coordination. These are the most important factors in homeland re-sponse — they are the key to achieving unity of effort. Without them, effective response is impossible.

Some recent and well-known major disasters illustrate the problem. Nuclear disasters elicit particularly grave concern because of their potential for large-scale human suffering and extremely long-term consequences. On April 26, 1986, the Chernobyl nuclear reactor in the former Soviet Republic of Ukraine experienced a disastrous explosion resulting from a combination of poor design and human error. While not an American catastrophe, Chernobyl affected people in many nations. It demonstrated clearly that problems with unity of effort are not unique to our system; the potential exists anytime multiple organizations and jurisdictions have to work together. It also shows the broad (even international) consequences of ineffective disaster response.

Soviet authorities tried to prevent news of it from reaching the rest of the world even as they struggled to respond to the crisis. The first notification came from radiation detectors at a Swedish nuclear facility more than 600 miles from the Chernobyl plant.[2] First responders desperately undertook suicidal efforts to control the fire, using inadequate equipment and techniques. The resulting cloud of radioactive material spread over much of Europe. Soviet attempts to hide the nature and extent of the problem overshadowed and hampered their internal response and precluded timely assistance from potential international partners, even as it put populations across their country and the region at risk. Ad hoc response and poorly coordinated efforts exacerbated the consequences of what is commonly acknowledged to be the worst disaster in the history of the nuclear industry.[3] Despite the bravery of those at the scene, both planning and response were ineffective; and the consequences of the disaster will continue to challenge the Ukrainian government and many others for decades to come.

On September 11, 2001 (9/11), terrorist cells of the al Qaeda network hijacked four commercial airliners. They flew two of them into the twin towers of the World Trade Center in New York. A third plane was used to attack the Pentagon in Arlington, Virginia, and the fourth crashed outside of Shanksville, Pennsylvania. Using comparatively low technology, a determined enemy was able to strike a substantial blow within the U.S. homeland. Nearly 3,000 people were killed, the largest single loss of life to foreign attack on American soil in the nation's history.[4] In the immediate crisis, authorities struggled to obtain an accurate picture of the situation, share information between agencies, and determine how to coordinate government efforts to respond to the attacks.[5] In the days and weeks that followed, senior leaders had extreme difficulty coordinating the vast resources and capabilities of the nation to mitigate and recover from the attacks, anticipate and prevent additional attacks, and develop an appropriate response.[6] Air Force planes flew combat patrols over the nation's cities and National Guardsmen patrolled the airports. Congress hastily debated and passed the USA PATRIOT Act. State and local governments desperately tried to evaluate their vulnerabilities and to protect the public and private assets in their jurisdictions. Substantial reorganizations in the federal government were quickly initiated. A new cabinet-level Department of Homeland Security was created by combining 22 federal agencies. The Department of Defense (DoD) established a new combatant command (U.S. Northern Command) to manage homeland defense, and created a new position with the title of Assistant Secretary of Defense for Homeland Defense and America's Security Affairs (ASD-HDASA). These changes were generally necessary and prudent, but unity of effort cannot be attained by simply redrawing a line and block chart. Unfortunately, some of these organizational changes had the unintended consequence of making unity of effort more difficult. Despite all the restructuring of agencies and refocusing of resources, many still question whether the nation is truly safer or better prepared for the next terrorist strike.[7]

Four years later, on August 29, 2005, Hurricane Katrina struck the Gulf Coast of Louisiana and Mississippi. The initial effects of the storm, coupled with levee failures in New Orleans, caused widespread devastation and flooding. Over the ensuing weeks, poor information sharing, lack of coordination, and politically-motivated bickering delayed a unified response, and thereby exacerbated the suffering of the affected population.[8] After Hurricane Katrina, another congressional inquiry detailed the causes and results of the most expensive natural disaster in U.S. history.[9] Despite massive national efforts over the preceding 4 years to reorganize, refocus, and better prepare, the congressional inquiry noted a lack of initiative, cooperative effort, effective communication, and situational awareness. Once again, unity of effort eluded us.

More recently, a large man-made disaster struck the same region. On April 20, 2010, a British Petroleum (BP) deep-water oil-drilling platform in the Gulf of Mexico known as Deepwater Horizon suffered a catastrophic explosion, sinking the rig. Eleven crew members lost their lives, and the damaged well spilled crude oil into the Gulf of Mexico as BP, its partners, the scientific and technical communities, and government leaders at all levels struggled to find ways to cap the well and contain the massive spill. The involvement of a major foreign-owned multinational corporation further complicated the situation. Over the next 3 months, the well discharged an estimated five million barrels of oil into the gulf, constituting the largest accidental oil spill in history and resulting in widespread ecological and economic distress that is being felt to this day.[10] While analyses are still being written, one might easily conclude that failure to achieve unity of effort reduced the effectiveness of the response, mitigation, and recovery efforts.

These major catastrophes differ in many of their particulars. Some mishaps that were preventable occurred; some that were unavoidable were made worse by human error, mechanical failures, procedural lapses, and poor information sharing. This monograph will not discuss in-depth postmortems on any of these disasters, as such. Rather, it provides recent and well-known examples of a common problem in disaster planning and response. Each crisis was characterized by multiple failures among the participants to work together effectively. Leaders charged with planning and managing the response failed to achieve unity of effort. They were less effective than they needed to be, and the loss of life, human suffering, and other long-term negative consequences were accordingly made considerably worse.

Disasters in our homeland have enormous consequences. Regardless of their cause, size, and scope, they always hold the potential for significant loss of life, human suffering, economic dislocation, and erosion of public confidence in our government and our leaders. Given what is at stake, we must do better. The findings of many investigatory committees and blue ribbon commissions underscore a broad consensus that there are substantial impediments to unity of effort and effective response. Such findings inform the ongoing national conversation on this topic, as well they should. This monograph proposes three recommendations for improving our capacity for unified effort in homeland response operations. Certainly there are other ways to enhance and synergize our response capabilities, but we believe these proposals merit careful consideration.

First, to be consistently effective, we must create a culture of collaboration and cooperation. We must establish the intellectual pre-conditions for unified effort by changing the way we think about homeland response. Creating an operating culture that fosters unity of effort requires a national homeland response *doctrine*, formulated in a dynamic and responsive *doctrinal system*. Our military forces and our national firefighting entity have such systems. The military's joint doctrine development system grew out of the legislative mandate of the Goldwater-Nichols Act,[11] while national fire doctrine has developed under the National Fire Administration, established in response to shortcomings identified in the 1973 report of the National Commission on Fire Prevention and Control.[12] However, the comprehensive doctrinal systems they have developed are not replicated to the same degree across the wider homeland response community.

More important, there is no single national doctrinal system that covers all functions and stakeholders. To be clear, there is published federal doctrine embodied in the National Response Framework (NRF), the National Incident Management System (NIMS), and the Incident Command System (ICS). Publication of these documents was a substantial step forward. But what is missing is far more important. Doctrine is dynamic; it is evolutionary. To be effective, it must develop within a common system, through a standardized process incorporating the inputs of all stakeholders as a timely response to the lessons of realistic training and operational experience. We propose that such a comprehensive doctrinal system is not only possible for homeland response, but in fact essential. It is the living structure and process through which a culture of cooperation and collaboration can be fostered.

Second, to implement a common national doctrine which operates across the many divides in our system, we need a new management construct, one that operates in the spaces between jurisdictions and functions to integrate and synergize the contributions of all. Again, our military has pointed a way forward. Several unified commands operate Joint Interagency Coordinating Groups (JIACGs) and Joint Interagency Task Forces (JIATFs).[13] The doctrinal basis for their organization and functions is slender but growing, and their operational effectiveness is well established. The results of JIATF-South over the preceding 2 decades, for example, provide clear evidence of the value of the concept.[14] We propose establishing a similar concept and rigorously testing it across the range of homeland response operations. The concept should not be a military one, but instead a more broadly construed doctrinal model which will evolve over time and encompass all elements involved in homeland response operations.

Third, we should remove the barriers to unity of effort within our military civil support capabilities. This requires that we put in place the authorities and doctrine necessary to provide our governors (and the President) with the ability to effectively employ DoD assets for homeland response. Most of our military—both active and reserve—contains capabilities with strong utility for civil support. Placing them off limits for homeland response is simply counterproductive. Our reserve components (RC) are particularly well positioned to bear principal responsibility for defense support of civil authority (DSCA); they are forward deployed across the nation. However, impediments to their training, resourcing, readiness, and availability for this mission remain. Military capabilities that might be useful to a governor should not be withheld in time of need, regardless of the command to which they are assigned. This requires that we build the authorities and processes necessary to access useful forces and capabilities, when and where they are needed. It may entail further modification of Title 32 of the U.S. code to permit swift and seamless movement of capabilities into a status accessible to a governor, and will certainly require improved procedural mechanisms.[15] Recent steps to clarify and simplify dual status command structures are a logical step in this direction.[16] We believe that many military capabilities could, under the right circumstances, be available to a governor and serve under a qualified dual status commander. Additionally, procedures for identifying and preparing capabilities in advance of catastrophe must be developed. DSCA is a complex mission set. Available forces should be designated and trained in advance if their capabilities are to be fully ready when called. States must be able to plan for homeland contingency operations with confidence, knowing which military capabilities are ready and available, and empowered to act decisively to employ them when needed.[17]

Why National Doctrine?

We must focus first on doctrine to enable unity of effort in homeland response. One might observe that we already have federal doctrine published by the

Department of Homeland Security, that the services have joint doctrine for civil support and homeland response, and that many elements across the various Emergency Support Functions (ESFs)[18] have a published doctrine. However, it is not the doctrine we possess, but rather the doctrine we lack which is at issue. The open questions about our homeland response capabilities, including those questions that have yet to be asked, must be answered with doctrinal solutions. For this to occur, we need a robust national homeland response doctrine which is more than a federal doctrine, larger than the doctrine of individual response functions or joint military civil response doctrine. It must subsume, deconflict, and integrate the separate doctrines of its members; it must do so responsively on a continuing basis. It must draw on the input and expertise of all participants, particularly the agencies and departments of the states and localities, and other nonfederal stakeholders. What currently exists is good but not unifying doctrine; and it is a federal doctrine only. A unifying national doctrine will incorporate all the capabilities of the nation within a single system.

The experience of our military makes a strong case for a national homeland response doctrine system. Despite organizationally similar cultures, unity of command, and strong service doctrine, our military's performance in operations such as the Iranian hostage rescue in 1980 and the Grenada intervention in 1983 underscore how difficult it is for complex organizations to work together effectively. In contrast, the impressive combat performances in Panama, Kuwait, Iraq, and Afghanistan in recent decades, and in many operations short of war in various locations, underscore the value of joint doctrine in creating unified effort across the services. Yet it took a statutory push—the

Goldwater-Nichols Act—to create the joint doctrine development system and the body of doctrine our military now employs. Prior to that legislation, there was no standard process for initiating, coordinating, approving, or revising joint doctrine. There was no requirement for congruity between joint and service doctrine, or for incorporating the requirements of the force commanders who had to employ the doctrine. There was no way to identify and address conceptual voids, and no mechanism for validating the efficacy of emerging concepts.[19] Our military forces—and the nation—paid dearly for the lack of a robust joint doctrine over the decades from the end of World War II through 1985.[20] Yet the military's joint doctrine system is now in place, has matured over the past 25 years, and continues to evolve. The benefits for the military services are demonstrated by their unrivaled performance across a broad range of operational challenges. Considering the thousands of disparate stakeholders involved in homeland response, it will certainly be more difficult to bring this kind of rigor to a national doctrinal system. For this very reason, such a system is all the more important.

Doctrine performs a vital unifying function in complex operations. It delineates "what is taught, believed, and advocated as what is right (i.e., what works best)." It provides textbook solutions for how things should be done to achieve specific results. It "standardizes terminology, training, relationships, responsibilities, and processes."[21] Prior to Goldwater-Nichols, the individual services had well-developed doctrinal concepts. Each had institutional structures for identifying unmet requirements and for updating and improving their doctrine. For example, the Army's doctrinal revolution following the Vietnam

War was an institutional response to perceived new strategic challenges. It helped lay the foundation for the successes of our land forces over the ensuing 3 decades.[22] Yet individual service doctrine, by definition, must be subordinate to joint doctrine. To achieve common understanding between the services, joint doctrine coordinates and integrates service doctrinal concepts. It operates across service boundaries to unify their approaches to common challenges and bind together the ways in which they are addressed. Joint doctrine provides the cultural basis for effective communication by standardizing terms and formats. It enhances coordination by generating and updating common tactics, techniques, and procedures (TTPs). It promotes collaboration and cooperation by providing common ways of thinking about and solving problems. Doctrine clarifies relationships: who leads and who follows, who supports and who is supported. Joint doctrine "promotes a common perspective from which to plan, train, and conduct military operations . . . it guides employment of forces in coordinated and integrated action toward a common objective."[23] Joint doctrine creates the basis for our military to cooperatively produce capabilities far greater than any single service can field. In short, despite the commonly acknowledged importance across the services of unity of command, it is joint doctrine that has given them unity of effort.

Joint military doctrine operates in a dynamic cycle. It provides a process through which capability gaps are identified. Corresponding operating concepts are developed, fielded, and incorporated into operational plans and then validated against rigorous standards in realistic training and the crucible of real-world experience. The results are analyzed and used to influence the ongoing development of doctrine. Successful results support training, organizing, and equipping standards. Failures are equally important, driving changes to improve doctrinal concepts and standards and hopefully future results. But whether success or failure, the development of future capabilities, of joint operating concepts, and of standards for equipping, training, and organizing response elements are dynamically affected by the rigorously tested results of today's doctrinal concepts.

A recent DoD advisory panel on enhancing defense support of civil authority found that "there is currently no comprehensive national integrated planning system to respond to either natural or manmade disasters." Further, "planning among federal agencies and other levels of government is fragmented and nonstandard, and there is no formal process by which state plans can inform federal planning and vice versa."[24] The panel report asserted that:

> the emergency response community has long understood that the foundation for any effective response to a . . . catastrophic incident consists of effective planning and information sharing before the emergency and a coordinated preparation and response activity prior to, during, and after the incident.[25]

To correct the shortcomings in planning and coordination processes, they recommended that:

> the President direct the establishment of an integrated planning system that promotes coordinated planning among local, state, and federal government entities and the private sector . . . international organizations and friendly and allied governments.[26]

The panel cited a 2003 Homeland Security Presidential Directive (HSPD-8) as an appropriate model. Much of what HSPD-8 sought to establish looks a lot like a national homeland response doctrine system. It directed the creation of:

- A national doctrine and planning guidance, instruction, and process to ensure consistent planning across the federal government;
- A mechanism for concept development;
- A process . . . for plan refinement which reflects developments in risk, capabilities, and policies, and incorporates lessons learned from exercises and actual incidents;
- A process that links regional, state, local, and tribal plans; planning cycles; and processes, and allows these plans to inform the development of federal plans;
- A process for fostering vertical and horizontal integration of federal, state, local, and tribal plans, and for using assessments of state, local, and tribal capabilities to inform the development of federal plans; and,
- A guide for all-hazards planning, with comprehensive, practical guidance and instruction on fundamental planning principles that can be used at federal, state, local, and tribal levels to assist the planning process.[27]

The objective of HSPD-8 was to create a system in which thinking about homeland response among federal, state, and local governments comes together to create a unified, and unifying, national way of operating—that is, a national doctrine. There is federal doctrine, and there are federal exercises and training; states and localities also plan and train. However, there is no national point of convergence in our homeland response thinking. There is no single place where differing concepts are understood, de-conflicted, and synthesized to create integrated response capabilities. There is no unified system to identify capability gaps and requirements, develop concepts, solicit input, and ensure "buy in" from all stakeholders. There is no systematic process to validate national doctrinal concepts in full-scale, realistic exercises, and real-world experience, or to integrate them into national planning. The effect of a robust joint operating doctrine on our military has been profound. It would be equally profound for our homeland response capabilities. It would provide a locus in which common understandings are formed, where common operating concepts and principles are analyzed, validated, updated, and authoritatively disseminated.

A National Homeland Response Doctrine System.

A system that dynamically develops a national homeland response doctrine for all participants is the critical first step to enabling unity of effort. But what should this system look like? In general, it should operate like the model depicted in Figure 1. It should certainly include all of the elements in HSPD-8 outlined above. The DoD advisory panel found that the current administration had not "reaffirmed, amended, or superseded" HSPD-8, and so they recommended a presidential directive establishing an integrated national planning system. Yet, a system founded on executive order seems inconsistent with creating the basis for unity of effort. The flaw in such a system, of course, is that it is a creature of the federal executive branch alone. It will extend only as far as the reach of the executive branch and last as long as a President directs. Presidential orders also lack specific and long-term funding, hampering their implementation beyond the executive branch.

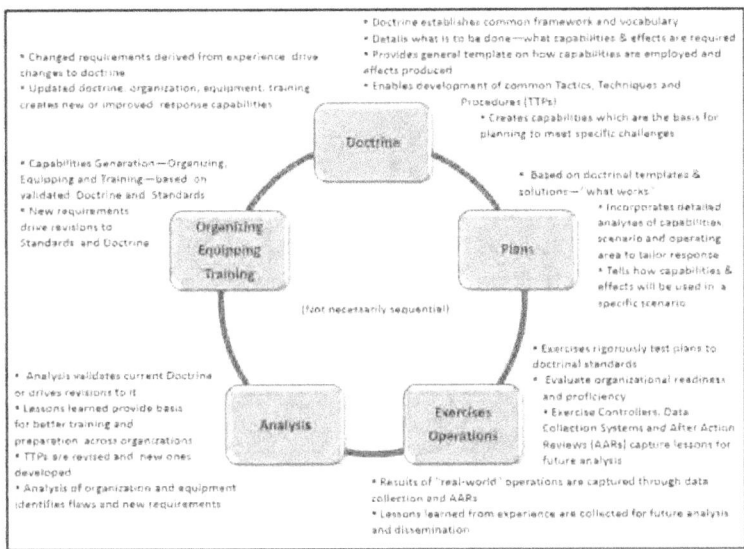

Figure 1. Theoretical Model of the National Homeland Response Doctrinal Cycle.

A truly national system must be based on more than executive fiat, and must endure beyond the next election cycle. It is important to start somewhere, and a presidential directive may be a useful starting point. Certainly, it could enable a doctrinal system to be established more quickly. But in the end, just as the armed forces needed the legislative spur of the Gold-water-Nichols Act to develop a true joint doctrine system, so a national homeland response doctrinal system will require a legislative impetus to be enduring, to be properly resourced and fully reflective of the broad mix of interests at stake. Just as important, this system must be larger than the federal government. In our democratic system, responsibility and authority are balanced. Our homeland response is graduated, beginning at the local level and progressively drawing upon the higher-level resources and capabilities needed to address the challenge. In this system, under most circumstances the federal government can lead, facilitate, incorporate, integrate . . . but not dictate. Consequently, it must include—as equal partners— the states, localities, and others. A congressional mandate would provide the kind of broad national representation that is needed. The executive branch could undertake both kinds of actions, initially issuing a presidential directive to the various executive branch departments even as legislation is developed to create a more lasting system. However, a national doctrine system will be enduring only if it is broadly construed, has a basis in federal law, and is adequately resourced. Most important, it must include more than federal government entities and equities.

Properly established, a national homeland response doctrinal system will incorporate a senior body of elected and appointed federal, state, and local officials who will validate requirements and emerging strategic operating concepts. Including representation from states, localities, and other players that must be a part of a national system will ensure their buy-in and cooperation. Operating below this senior level should be a set of institutional bodies which identify capability gaps and requirements, develop draft doctrinal concepts, present them for validation, and, once validated, fully develop and implement them as interagency and/or intergovernmental components of the national doctrine. This subordinate structure should also include regular representation and input from all members of the homeland response community. National doctrine should begin with and build upon the NRF, NIMS, and ICS, which are well accepted and broadly understood; it would develop and evolve concepts as needed. Doctrinal concepts created in this system would be incorporated into planning at each level in part because the stakeholders help to develop them. The system could further ensure this by including procedures for linking local, state, and federal plans, planning cycles and processes, and for integrating plans of other stakeholders into federal planning. This will require more than a new process — it will require a doctrinally-based awareness that the federal government must (in most cases) lead by supporting. It will require federal response plans that support and integrate those of the states and other participants in the process.

A national doctrine system must go beyond concept development and integration of plans. Doctrinal concepts, plans, and capabilities must be rigorously tested with realistic training and exercises, conducted under consistent standards relying on objective data collection, and combined with painstaking analysis of actual, "real world" operations. Validation of doctrine should include a national homeland response training center system, with its main "training aid" being an actual mock-up of a small city.[28] This unfortunate city would be routinely threatened by natural disasters, assaulted by imaginative domestic and foreign terrorists, subject to industrial accidents, and bathed in pandemic diseases. It would host a diverse array of participants drawn from the federal interagency, state and local governments, and other relevant partners. A full-scale national training center would be a proving ground for developing doctrinal concepts that can be replicated, trained, improved, adapted, and applied in jurisdictions, agencies, and organizations across the nation. It should link multiple elements and smaller regional centers in virtual space to provide tailored and multiechelon training across agencies, jurisdictions, and responsibilities. Senior leaders of federal, state, and local government would interact with news media, industry, and private organizations while directing and managing actual responders operating in realistic conditions. The system should be robustly instrumented and staffed to gather data for analysis, dissemination, and doctrinal development. The result would be better response elements, led by better trained and more capable leaders — in particular those senior leaders responsible for achieving unified effort across jurisdictions and response functions. Doctrinal concepts would be validated, improved, or rejected. Results would be passed into a feedback loop which would provide the basis for improvements in training, organization, equipment, and in the evolution of homeland response doctrine and capabilities.

The "integrated planning system" envisioned in HSPD-8 is important, and if fully implemented could certainly improve unity of effort. But, we should not focus solely on plans, which can and should change. Plans and planning are vitally important, but a national doctrine is larger than the plans it produces. Consistent unity of effort will grow out of a culture of cooperation and collaboration, which can be fostered by a national doctrine system. Plans specify ways of doing things, but doctrine begins with ways of thinking and understanding — these should precede and drive planning. A national homeland response doctrine system would integrate all stakeholders in the evolutionary process of how we think about and understand challenges to safety and security at home, and collaboratively develop responses to them. It takes a great deal of time and effort to create an operational culture that fosters unity of effort. The example of our military's organizational evolution from the National Defense Reorganization Act of 1947, to the Goldwater-Nichols Act of 1986, to the present day, is instructive in this respect. Developing a culture of collaboration and cooperation for homeland response will not occur overnight, but rather as the long-term result of patient development and continuous improvement.

A New Management Construct.

A second way to achieve unity of effort is to improve our management capabilities. With the advent of a dynamic national homeland response doctrinal system, we will need to develop a new management structure that will operate in the spaces between agencies and organizations. The NRF and ICS identify unified command as a key principle for effective incident management, but it is a temporary, incident-specific creation rather than a permanent one. Unity of command can be temporarily achieved in any incident, but cannot be permanently maintained, nor would we want it to be, in a system based on graduated response and shared responsibility. What we want to do, both within the scope of a single incident and as an ongoing factor in planning and preparation, is to establish and sustain unified effort. Day to day, our departments and agencies do not work together, yet in a crisis, they must. A national doctrine will provide the basis for effectively working together by establishing the intellectual pre-conditions for cooperation, collaboration, communication, and coordination. However, given the breadth and scope of what is to be implemented, a new management construct must also be created, one that works to bridge the divides within the homeland response community before, during, and after incidents. It must foster unified effort across the doctrine development cycle, throughout planning and plan integration, and in training, organizing, and equipping response capabilities. The national homeland response doctrine system will function in an interagency, intergovernmental, multijurisdictional environment. Implementing it requires a permanent management structure that will similarly operate in the gaps between agencies and governments. Here too, the experience of our military provides an example that points in the direction homeland response must go: the Joint Interagency Task Force, or JIATF.

Joint military doctrine for civil support has recognized the need for interagency planning and coordination for a number of years. This doctrine described an Interagency Planning Cell (IPC) that is "activated upon receipt of the . . . warning or alert order, or at the direction of the combatant commander" in response to a domestic disaster. This ad hoc entity was tailored to the crisis and set up to "rapidly advise the supported combatant commander about the resources of other agencies in the relief effort." The concept was developed to facilitate "coherent and efficient planning and coordination effort through the participation of interagency subject matter experts, [and to lighten the] burden of coordination at the JTF level."[29] In this way, the IPC functioned similarly to the interagency Catastrophic Disaster Response Group (CDRG) called for under the Federal Emergency Management Agency (FEMA) doctrine. A CDRG "convenes . . . when needed" at the headquarters of the Department of Homeland Security (DHS). Comprised of representatives from various federal agencies, the CDRG is set up to "provide guidance and policy direction on coordination and operational issues."[30] Such interagency coordination entities are important, but both the IPC and CDRG—and similar ad hoc organizations—are temporary.

More recently, joint military doctrine has promulgated the concept of a standing JIACG. The JIACG is a permanent planning and coordination element. Described as "an element of a [geographic combatant commander's] staff," the JIACG "is an interagency staff group that establishes and enhances regular, timely, and collaborative working relationships between other governmental agencies' representatives and military operational planners." The JIACG is established at the discretion of the combatant commander to "complement the interagency coordination that occurs at the national level through the DoD and the NSC [National Security Council] and HSC [Homeland Security Council] systems." Its members "participate in contingency, crisis action, and security cooperation planning, [and] provide a conduit back to their parent organizations."[31] This helps synchronize joint operations—of the combatant command—with the efforts of other government agencies. As a more permanent element, the JIACG is an improvement over the IPC and CDRG. Yet it is still optional and, more importantly, an adjunct to military planning and operations. It incorporates other federal agencies and even nongovernmental organizations (NGOs) and inter-governmental organizations (IGOs), but these function under military direction, to support military needs.

A more germane example is provided by JIATF-South. Established more than 2 decades ago to coordinate military and interagency efforts to combat the international narcotics trade, JIATF-South has built a strong reputation for success. Although established under authority of the National Defense Authorization Act of 1989 and still nominally a military entity, JIATF-South is much more a multiservice, multiagency national task force. A key element in this entity is the integration of participating agencies in command and leadership posts. It is led by a Coast Guard admiral, with a deputy director from the Customs and Border Patrol (CPB). It integrates senior leaders from various federal agencies into its leadership structure at lower levels as well: the senior intelligence and operations directors are military officers, but their deputies come from the Drug Enforcement Administration (DEA) and the CPB. In routine operations, "it is not uncommon to see a CBP agent serving as command duty officer, an Air Force captain as the intelligence watch officer, a Coast Guard operations specialist as the intelligence watch assistant, and a Navy lieutenant as the tactical action officer."[32] JIATF-South incorporates multiple agencies into its intelligence operations, effectively sharing information drawn from the resources of its members. It also includes international liaisons. The joint service, multiagency, and international structure enables it to quickly develop and share fused operational information, task assets under the control of the combatant commander, and coordinate the efforts of other assets under the control of participating agencies and international partners. While there is little formal military doctrine about what a JIATF is and should do—and virtually none among other participating agencies—the record of JIATF-South demonstrates that the concept works. As joint doctrine evolves, it will only strengthen and expand the potential of the JIATF.

There have been recent calls to establish JIATF-like entities for homeland response operations. For example, a recent advisory panel recommended formation of a JIATF for incidents involving chemical, biological, radiological, nuclear, or high-yield explosive (CBRNE) weapons, to facilitate "pre-incident planning and coordination" and rapidly "translate national-level decisionmaking for a CBRNE incident into operational and tactical actions."[33] Such ideas suggest an emerging consensus that the JIATF construct has utility in homeland response operations. Yet this and similar ideas, and the structure of even highly successful JIATFs like JIATF-South, are too narrowly construed at present. This interagency coordinating structure cannot, for example, be an adjunct of U.S. Northern Command (NORTHCOM). NORTHCOM has a role to play, with important lead responsibilities for homeland defense and support responsibilities for other homeland security and civil support operations. However, the structure that is needed cannot be subordinate to any particular federal agency or department—it must belong to and support them all. It must begin as a broadly held doctrinal concept, and become more robust through expansion of its potential. A standing JIATF-like interagency coordination and action group—an "ICAG" perhaps—should be established at the national level to integrate the planning, resourcing, and management of homeland response operations. It should reflect a common doctrinal understanding for a multi-participant entity operating in the spaces between agencies. As such, it cannot be a military structure, although it will certainly contain military elements. By the same token, it cannot be a creature of any other single agency or department head. The ICAG could rely on a lead agency for support, but because it serves to integrate the interagency space, it must draw on the capabilities and strengths of all relevant participants.

This model clearly has a similar application for the states. Each has a vigorous interagency community that is relevant to its own disaster planning and response efforts. If a federal ICAG would work to enhance unity of effort across the federal interagency, so too would a set of state-level ICAGs, accredited to each governor, perform the same useful function. One need not be overly prescriptive about the ICAG structure—the senior leader it serves should be free to tailor and employ it as suits the needs of his agencies and constituencies. As it evolves, the doctrinal concept might include narrow functional versions (e.g., an ICAG for national CBRNE response), as well as geographically based and broadly responsive ones—much as we have geographic and functional commands within our military to address different types of problems and responsibilities. In any case, some functions and characteristics should be common to all. These would include:

- Accreditation to a senior executive with authority over the interagency construct being coordinated, and accountable to the citizens served by the participating agencies and organizations;
- An integrated leadership structure that fosters full involvement by all participating agencies;
- Authority to task some assets useful to its routine work; and to coordinate for swift access to other assets that ought to be available when needed;
- Interagency analysis, fusion, and dissemination of relevant intelligence and operational information;

- Fair sharing of responsibilities for resourcing, staffing, and support; and even-handed treatment of the metrics of success for all participants;
- Ongoing coordination, communication, and collaboration between agencies served by the ICAG, as well as with the ICAGs of other states and the federal government.

Additional capabilities could be built into the ICAG concept. Over time, it would mature within the national homeland response doctrine; as governments at each level discover what works best, this information will be fed back into the doctrinal cycle to improve it. But regardless of how the ICAG is structured in each specific instance, it will operate with overarching responsibility, day in and day out, to be the integrating structure for all interagency participants, ensuring unity of effort in planning and operations.

Unity of Effort across the Military.

A third way to increase unity of effort is to improve our ability to employ all relevant military forces and functions in the full range of homeland response operations. Although its primary responsibility is defense against foreign threats, our military has taken on a wide range of other tasks in recent history, including nation-building,[34] stability operations,[35] and civil support.[36] Regarding the latter, the 2008 Commission on the National Guard and Reserves (CNGR) final report included a number of significant findings—among them, that DoD fails to put adequate effort (planning, programming, and budgeting) into civil support capabilities, and "historically has not made civil support a priority."[37]

It is somewhat ironic that our military would place less emphasis on support for civil authority at home, even as they have very successfully executed peace-keeping and stability operations abroad. In recent decades, both unilaterally and within multinational coalitions, our forces have routinely been the only entity capable of providing security and stability, preserving life and property, delivering medical care, and assisting in the restoration of civil institutions. Yet aside from National Guard operations, DoD has been reluctant to engage in civil support operations at home, and perhaps understandably so. There is substantial primary capability in our nation, at many levels, for disaster planning and response; state and local leaders are quite rightly held to account for their performance in this area. Yet the CNGR report recommends that Congress mandate civil support as a primary mission for DoD, "equal in priority to its combat responsibilities."[38]

The reason for this is plain: our military possesses a variety of capabilities with great value in responding to disasters and mitigating their effects; Americans expect that the military resources they paid for will be available when needed to protect them. It makes little difference to the injured, hungry, and dispossessed that the cause of their misery is a hurricane, a pandemic, an industrial disaster, or a terrorist strike. Their reasonable expectation is that "the government" will provide for public safety in their hour of need. For this reason, we should be removing impediments to unity of effort in utilizing our military forces, and our reserve components in particular, for homeland response operations when they are not engaged in federal missions overseas.

There are clear legal restrictions on the roles and uses of our military at home, which exist for sound reasons that need not be debated here.[39] It is sufficient to note that our forefathers wisely saw the problems inherent to employing military forces in roles normally confined to civil authority. However, the principal challenge in employing our military for homeland response is not a constitutional issue, but rather one of lesser law. The role of the federal government in raising, supporting, and employing military forces for both overseas missions and in various roles at home is clearly established, as is its ability to federalize National Guard units when needed. What is not well settled — but must be — is the ability of our governors to swiftly and seamlessly employ all the capabilities that might be made available to them when needed. This includes employment of military capabilities; it is critical to a governor's ability to formulate complete and well-coordinated homeland response plans with confidence. The status of most forces under Title 10 currently precludes placing them under state authority. This includes all DoD reserve components other than the National Guard and the active components of all services.

Most of our military capabilities are organized and resourced for federal service, as it ought to be. Yet some (the National Guard) are available for local and state missions. From a governor's standpoint, nothing could be easier or more efficient than having all the available military forces in his state operate under his control when not needed for federal missions. There are sound reasons why this is not so, and our present system — despite the Title 10/Title 32 divide — has served reasonably well over time in providing ready forces for federal missions. Certainly, no one could claim that National Guard forces have been less ready or available for service overseas since September 2001 than their Title 10 counterparts because they were tasked with state missions. In fact, quite the opposite is true. The example of the governor of Louisiana doing without thousands of that state's National Guard soldiers who were deployed to Iraq during Hurricane Katrina simply underscores the point that when the nation is at war, our military forces are at the federal government's direction. What has become increasingly clear since 9/11 is that state and local jurisdictions have a vital role to play in the full range of homeland response operations, including preventing and responding to terrorism. Given this reality, how might we reorganize to broaden the base of military capabilities available to them?

The CNGR made several recommendations to improve military support for homeland response. It recognized the value of new capabilities (such as National Guard homeland response elements), as well as other military units which are "dual-capable forces."[40] Not all military forces have a value in civil support operations. Some have more obvious uses than others, but many are, in fact, dual-capable. This includes not only National Guard, but Title 10 active and reserve forces as well. These elements have routinely served in peacekeeping and stability operations overseas and occasionally in support of civil authority at home, performing tasks which are not the ones for which they were originally organized, trained, and equipped. Simply put, our military can do more than just fight our nation's wars. From the birth of the republic to the present day, our National Guard—and on occasion, our Title 10 forces—have proven the value of dual-capable military forces.

Achieving unity of effort for homeland response among our military services is neither a matter of determining which forces ought to be in the National Guard and which should not, nor one of simply combining National Guard and Reserve structures (an argument which begs the point). Rather, it is one of determining when and how to best place military forces under a governor's authority to make them readily available for civil support roles. Toward this end, we should be removing impediments to training, planning for, and employing military units under the direction of a governor. A pre-qualified dual status commander would have authority to direct and coordinate the efforts of all military forces acting in support of the governor (or the governors) of affected states and territories. These officers are senior military leaders trained and selected in advance for their expertise and local knowledge. This positions them well to plan for the utilization of available military assets in their regions. Dual status command has been successfully employed in recent years for pre-planned joint and multiagency civil support events such as the 2004 G8 Summit, nominating conventions, and border control operations.[41] It makes sense for the military leaders with the most local knowledge and experience to lead defense support of civil authority in their areas of responsibility. Dual status command works. It should be the rule, not the exception; and better methods must be developed for placing useful military capabilities under dual status command, when requested and if available, for homeland response. This means developing better advance planning and implementation procedures for dual status command, such as has been proposed by the Council of Governors.[42] This should include the full range of "no notice" homeland response disaster events.

We must also make all relevant military capabilities available for homeland response in a way that facilitates effective planning. The services have developed procedures for identification and rotation of forces to support overseas deployments, such as the Army Force Generation (ARFORGEN) model. This system is a "rotational readiness model" which provides "strategic flexibility to meet security requirements for a continuous presence of deployed forces."[43] Such a system could be adapted to identify capabilities available for civil support operations in a similar way—a civil support force generation cycle—to ensure that those who plan for civil support by DoD assets have a predictable way to obtain needed capabilities to support those plans and contingencies. This would facilitate early identification and training of units and capabilities—active and reserve—for civil support task proficiency as they rotate into the pool of available elements; and it could be nuanced to complement and support the demands of federal missions overseas. With a predictable system for force generation, governors and dual status commanders would be in a better position to plan for, request, and employ available military capabilities when they are needed.

Unity of Effort.

The greatest challenge in homeland response operations is creating unity of effort. Many essential capabilities are spread across multiple jurisdictions, agencies, and organizations. This patchwork of authority, responsibility, and capability reflects our vibrant democratic system, yet it is these same divides that makes unity of effort so difficult. Most of the time, we want these seams in our system. We prefer to deal

with governments close to home, accessible and responsive to most of our routine needs. In times of crisis, we do not want federal authority to replace state
and local authority. But we do want our governments
to work together, to use assets and capabilities that are
already available in coordinated and thoughtful ways
to ensure the public safety. When necessary, we want
federal assets to complement and complete — not com-
pete with — our local and state efforts in a seamless,
unified response.

This requires a new approach. It requires us to
foster a culture of communication, coordination, collaboration, and cooperation among the many entities
that have a role in homeland response operations. To
be able to act with unity and decision, we must be able
to plan, train, resource, and prepare for unified effort.
This begins with how we think about homeland response, and each participant's role in it. A truly unifying national doctrine that stresses these tenets, developed and dynamically updated in an inclusive system,
will break down barriers to effectiveness and remove
impediments to unity of effort in times of crisis. To
implement a national doctrine across the divides in
our system, we need new management concepts that
work between and among all participants, such as the
proposed interagency coordination and action group.
This element will integrate and synthesize the efforts
of all stakeholders, working in the spaces between to
stitch together the jurisdictional patchwork into a us-
able blanket of protection. We must remove all barriers that currently exist to full utilization of relevant
military capabilities for homeland response. This can
be accomplished by making forces available to our
governors when and where they are needed, return-
ing them to the nation when the crisis is past; and by

providing reliable processes to plan for their readiness and availability before disaster strikes.

Achieving unity of effort in homeland response is a complex challenge, among the greatest of our age. It is the single most important factor in our ability to plan for and respond effectively to disasters in our homeland. We devote enormous resources to public safety and security at many levels. Our citizens surely have a right to expect that these resources will be well used by their leaders, elected and appointed. This means that we must find better ways to work together. It requires leaders and organizations at all levels to combine their efforts, resources, and capabilities to achieve responsive and complete solutions. John Jay observed in the *Federalist Papers No. 3* that "among the many objects to which a wise and free people find it necessary to direct their attention, that of providing for their safety seems to be the first."[44] There cannot be any higher priority for government than ensuring the safety of its citizens. This is a serious issue, deserving a serious approach. National security begins with homeland security, and homeland security depends fundamentally on our ability to work together, to bring our enormous capacity to bear at the right time, the right place, and in the right measure. Americans have long and proud traditions both of celebrating our differences, and of joining together in adversity to achieve common purposes. We should not allow any of the routinely divisive factors prevent us from working together effectively in times of crisis.

ENDNOTES

1. Carl Von Clausewitz, *On War*, Michael Howard and Peter Paret, eds. and trans., Princeton, NJ: Princeton University Press, pp. 119-121.

2. "Chernobyl Haunts Engineer Who Alerted the World," CNN World News Interactive, April 26, 1996, available from *www.cnn.com/WORLD/9604/26/chernobyl/230pm/index2.html*.

3. "Chernobyl's Legacy: Health, Environmental and Socio-Economic Impacts," The Chernobyl Forum: 2003-2005, Vienna, Austria: International Atomic Energy Agency Division of Publications, p. 10, available from *www.iaea.org/Publications/Booklets/Chernobyl/chernobyl.pdf*.

4. U.S. Congress, "Report of the National Commission on Terrorist Attacks upon the United States," *The 9/11 Commission Report*, Washington, DC: U.S. Government Printing Office, p. 311, available from *www.9-11commission.gov/report/911Report.pdf*.

5. The 9/11 *Commission Report* details multiple examples of chaos and confusion during the morning of the attacks, at every level from the federal interagency down to the local level, such as the interaction between the New York Port Authority and the tenants in the World Trade Center. It cites problems with information sharing and attaining situational awareness, for example, between the North American Aerospace Defense Command (NORAD) and the Federal Aviation Administration (FAA); and in attempting to put fighter aircraft into the air (*ibid.*, pp. 26-27) to respond to attacking aircraft. Another example was the failure of the Port Authority to develop fire evacuation protocols, to convey those to Trade Center tenants, and to ensure that the tenants had been adequately oriented (*ibid.*, pp. 280-281). Recent releases of audio tapes from the morning of the attack bear out the report's findings, particularly "confusion and lack of co-ordination between military and civil authorities in the aftermath of the attacks." See Karen McVeigh, "Newly Released 9/11 Audio Recordings Reveal Chaos and Confusion," *guardian.co.uk*, London, United Kingdom (UK), September 8, 2011, available from *www.guardian.co.uk/world/2011/sep/08/september-11-audio-recordings-public*.

6. *The 9/11 Commission Report*, pp. 325-328.

7. Ten years after 9/11, stories appear routinely in the media about potential terrorist threats. As the anniversary of the terrorist strikes approached, there was increased concern of another attack by al Qaeda. For example, the *Chicago Sun-Times* reported that "The U.S. government has long known that terrorists see the 10th anniversary of 9/11 and other uniquely American dates as opportunities to strike. Officials have also been concerned that some may see this anniversary as an opportunity to avenge Osama bin Laden's death." Eileen Sullivan and Lolita C. Baldor, "Threat Puts New York, DC on alert as 9/11 Anniversary Nears," *Chicago Sun-Times*, September 10, 2011, from *www.suntimes.com/news/nation/7568755-418/terror-threat-puts-ny-dc-on-alert-as-911-anniversary-nears.html*. Numerous opinion columns also speculate that the nation may not be safer. For example, a commentator recently wrote that "those who follow the terrorist threat most closely don't think bin Laden's death will have reduced it much, if at all." Christopher Dickey, "The Next Terror Threat," *The Daily Beast*, May 6, 2011, available from *www.thedailybeast.com/articles/2011/05/06/al-qaeda-terror-threat-to-new-york-city-and-us-trains-remains-high.html*.

8. U.S. Congress, "Report by the Select Bipartisan Committee to Investigate the Preparation for and Response to Hurricane Katrina," *A Failure of Initiative*, Washington, DC: U.S. Government Printing Office, pp. 359-362.

9. *Ibid.*, p. 7.

10. Campbell Robertson and Clifford Krauss, "Gulf Spill Is the Largest of Its Kind, Scientists Say," *www.NYTimes.com*, August 2, 2010, available from *www.nytimes.com/2010/08/03/us/03spill.html*.

11. David A. Sawyer, "The Joint Doctrine Development System," *Joint Force Quarterly*, Winter 1996-97, pp. 36-37. The Goldwater-Nichols Department of Defense Reorganization Act of 1986 caused a far-reaching reorganization of the national defense establishment, viewed by many as the most significant since the National Security Act of 1947. Among its major provisions, it significantly strengthened the authority of the Chairman of the Joint Chiefs of Staff relative to the separate service chiefs. The act designated the Chairman as "the principal military advisor to the presi-

dent, National Security Council and secretary of defense." It also established the position of vice-chairman, made the Joint Staff the chairman's staff, and streamlined the operational chain of command from the president through the Secretary of Defense to the unified commanders. Regarding joint doctrine, the act vested statutory responsibility in the Chairman of the Joint Chiefs of Staff for "developing doctrine for the joint employment of the armed forces" (Title 10 U.S. Code Subtitle A Part I Chapter 5 § 153). Text available from *www.ndu.edu/library/goldnich/goldnich.html*.

12. Lennard G. Kruger, *United States Fire Administration: An Overview*, Washington, DC: Congressional Research Service, October 10, 2008, available from *opencrs.com/document/RS20071/2011-04-20/*.

13. *Joint Publication (JP) 3-57, Civil-Military Operations*, Washington, DC: Department of Defense, July 8, 2008, p. IV-12. A Joint Interagency Coordination Group (JIACG) is a staff group "composed of U.S. Government civilian and military experts." It "establishes regular, timely, and collaborative working relationships between civilian and military operational planners." The JIACG is "accredited [to the] combatant commander" and "tailored to meet [his] requirements." It enhances the combatant commander's ability to "collaborate at the operational level" with other federal agencies. Joint Interagency Task Forces (JIATFs) were developed during the Clinton Administration in an effort to correct perceived weaknesses in the command and control of the nation's counternarcotics efforts. As a result, four JIATFs were established (JIATF-North, -South, -East and -West) to better integrate the efforts of the federal interagency in narcotics interdiction. Along with military personnel, the JIATFs include staff from the U.S. Customs and Border Patrol (CBP), Federal Bureau of Investigation (FBI), Drug Enforcement Administration (DEA), Defense Intelligence Agency (DIA), and Department of State.

14. JIATF-South is located in Key West, Florida, and operates under the authority of U.S. Southern Command (USSOUTH-COM). Its mission is to "conduct interagency and international Detection & Monitoring operations," and to "facilitate the interdiction of illicit [narcotics] trafficking and other Narco-terrorist threats in support of national and partner nation security," available from *www.jiatfs.southcom.mil/*.

15. Title 32 of the U.S. Code lays out the legal basis for the National Guard. National Guard units are unique among the United States military in their dual status as both state and federal forces. While they are principally supported by federal funds, they remain under the command of the governor of the state until "federalized" (i.e., placed into federal service under Title 10 of the U.S. Code). Since National Guard forces are under the command of the governor while in Title 32 status, they are easily made available for tasks as directed by the governor (including training and readiness preparations for state missions). National Guardsmen may also be placed in "State Active Duty" status, in which the state pays their operating costs and utilizes them as needed to support other civil authorities. The National Guard provides civil support in thousands of missions each year. For example, in 2005—the year of Hurricane Katrina—the Army National Guard responded to over 23,000 incidents within the United States, including relief from tornadoes, wildfires, hurricanes, floods, and other natural and man-made disasters (National Guard Bureau, "Army National Guard Fact Sheet—Army National Guard 2005," Arlington, VA: available from *www.arng.army.mil/SiteCollection-Documents/Publications/News%20Media%20Factsheets/ARNG_Factsheet_May_06%20ARNG%20fact%20Sheet.pdf*).

16. Jeffrey W. Burkett, "Command and Control of Military Forces in the Homeland," *Joint Force Quarterly,* Fall 2008, pp. 130-131. Under the 2004 National Defense Authorization Act, Congress amended Title 32 of the U.S. Code to permit National Guard officers to retain their state commissions after being ordered to federal active duty. This is known as dual status. In dual status command, a National Guard commander in Title 32 status is ordered to federal active duty under Title 10 but retains his state commission as well. This provides the statutory authority for one person to simultaneously command both state (Title 32 and state active duty status) and federal (Title 10 active and reserve) forces.

17. JP 5-0, *Joint Operation Planning,* Washington, DC: Department of Defense, August 11, 2011, p. GL-7. A contingency is a "situation requiring military operations in response to natural disasters, terrorists, subversives, or as otherwise directed by appropriate authority to protect U.S. interests." A contingency operation is "a military operation that: a. is designated by the Secretary

of Defense as an operation in which members of the Armed Forces are or may become involved in military actions, operations, or hostilities against an enemy of the United States or against an opposing force; or b. is created by definition of law." Department of Defense, JP 1, *Doctrine for the Armed Forces of the United States*, Washington, DC: U.S. Government Printing Office, May 2, 2007 (with Change 1, May 20, 2009), p. GL-6.

18. *National Response Framework*, Washington, DC: Department of Homeland Security, January 2008. The National Response Framework organizes federal and state response capabilities into 15 Emergency Support Functions (ESFs). The ESFs enable grouping functions and resources into similar categories to facilitate their employment and management. The ESFs "serve as the primary operational-level mechanism to provide assistance in functional areas such as transportation, communications, public works and engineering, firefighting, mass care, housing, human services, public health and medical services, search and rescue, agriculture and natural resources, and energy" (pp. 57-60).

19. David A. Sawyer, "The Joint Doctrine Development System," *Joint Force Quarterly*, Winter 1996-97, p. 37.

20. There are a range of historical examples demonstrating the problems inherent in working without a strong joint doctrine. One of the most persuasive is the failed attempt to rescue American hostages from Iran in 1980. The conclusions of the Holloway Report found that "the ad hoc nature of the organization and planning [was] related to most of the major issues" which contributed to the failure of the mission. "Report of the Special Operations Review Group," Washington, DC: Department of Defense, The Pentagon, 1980, p. 60.

21. Chairman of the Joint Chiefs of Staff Instruction (CJCSI) 5120.02B, *Joint Doctrine Development System*, Washington, DC: Department of Defense, The Pentagon, December 4, 2009, Appendix A, pp. 1-2.

22. U.S. Army Training and Doctrine Command, *Transforming the Army: TRADOC's First Thirty Years 1973-2003*, TRADOC Historical Study Series, Fort Monroe, VA: Military History Office, 2003, pp. 34-38.

23. JP 1, p. ix.

24. Steve Abbott, *et al.*, "Report of the Advisory Panel on Department of Defense Capabilities for Support of Civil Authorities After Certain Incidents to the Secretary of Defense and the Chairmen and Ranking Minority Members, Committees on Armed Services, U.S. Senate and U.S. House of Representatives," *Before Disaster Strikes: Imperatives for Enhancing Defense Support to Civil Authorities*, Washington, DC: U.S. Government Printing Office, September 15, 2010, pp. 28-29.

25. *Ibid.*, p. 35.

26. *Ibid.*, p. 29.

27. George W. Bush, Homeland Security Presidential Directive 8, *National Preparedness*, Annex 1, Washington, DC: The White House, December 17, 2003, available from *www.dhs.gov/xabout/laws/gc_1215444247124.shtm.*

28. A "full-scale" training center should be large enough to fully train and operate all participants in relevant scenarios. By way of comparison, the Army's National Training Center (NTC) at Fort Irwin, California, which opened in October 1980, is approximately the size of Rhode Island. See Anne W. Chapman, *The National Training Center Matures 1985-1993*, U.S. Army Training and Doctrine Command, TRADOC Historical Study Series, Fort Monroe, VA: Military History Office, 2003, p. 102. As the center matured, even this size was deemed insufficient for full-scale training, and additional land was sought (*Ibid.*, pp. 65-97). A National Homeland Response Training Center should emulate the military NTC in scale, scope, and capability.

29. JP 3-08, *Interagency Coordination during Joint Operations, Vol. I*, Washington, DC: Department of Defense, U.S. Government Printing Office, October 9, 1996, pp. III-3-III-5.

30. Department of Homeland Security, "Federal Response Plan," Washington, DC: U.S. Government Printing Office, January 2003, Appendix D.

31. JP 1, pp. VII-5-VII-7.

32. Richard M. Yeatman, "JIATF-South: Blueprint for Success," *Joint Force Quarterly*, Spring 1996-97, p. 26.

33. Abbott *et al.*, pp. 26-27.

34. James Dobbins *et al.*, "The Beginners Guide to Nation-Building," Santa Monica, CA: The RAND Corporation, National Security Research Division, 2007, p. xvii. The term "nation building" has been used in various ways. "Nation-building, as it is commonly referred to in the United States, involves the use of armed force as part of a broader effort to promote political and economic reforms with the objective of transforming a society emerging from conflict into one at peace with itself and its neighbors."

35. JP 3-0, *Joint Operations*, August 11, 2011, Washington, DC: U.S. Government Printing Office, p. V-4. Stability operations is "an umbrella term for various military missions, tasks, and activities conducted outside the United States in coordination with other instruments of national power to maintain or reestablish a safe and secure environment, and to provide essential governmental services, emergency infrastructure reconstruction, and humanitarian relief."

36. JP 3-28, *Civil Support*, September 14, 2007, Washington, DC: Department of Defense, U.S. Government Printing Office, pp. vii-x. The term "civil support" (CS) includes DoD support to U.S. civil authorities for domestic emergencies, and for designated law enforcement and other activities. "CS operations are divided into three broad categories of domestic emergencies, designated law enforcement support, and other activities." Domestic emergencies include disasters in which military capabilities are used to "save lives, prevent suffering, and mitigate great property damage under imminently serious conditions." It may include "assistance in restoring public health and services, and civil order may include augmentation of local first responders and equipment." Law enforcement support may include support for or augmentation of local law enforcement capabilities. Other activities include military operations in support of National Special Security Events (NSSE). NSSE are "certain special events that, by virtue of their

political, economic, social, or religious significance, may be the target of terrorism or other criminal activity."

37. Commission on the National Guard and Reserves, "Final Report to the Congress and the Secretary of Defense," *Transforming the National Guard and Reserves into a 21st Century Operational Force*," Washington, DC: U.S. Government Printing Office, January 31, 2008, p. 90.

38. *Ibid.*, p. 91.

39. Jennifer K. Elsea, *The Use of Federal Troops for Disaster Assistance*, Washington, DC: Congressional Research Service, U.S. Government Printing Office, September 16, 2005, available from *fpc.state.gov/documents/organization/53685.pdf*.

> Recognizing the risk that a standing army could pose to individual civil liberties and the sovereignty retained by the several states, but also cognizant of the need to provide for the defense of the nation against foreign and domestic threats, the framers of the Constitution incorporated a system of checks and balances to divide the control of the military between the President and Congress and to share the control of the militia with the states.

The Posse Comitatus Act of 1878 (18 U.S.C. section 1385: *Use of Army and Air Force as Posse Comitatus*) was passed to limit domestic law enforcement roles the Army had assumed in the post-Civil War era. However, its limitations have been gradually reduced as federal military forces have been employed in countering the international narcotics trade, and more recently, the threat of terrorism. Additionally, limitations of the Posse Comitatus Act never applied to military activity other than law enforcement (e.g., disaster response), nor to the National Guard while serving under a governor in Title 32 status. (See, for example, Craig T. Trebilcock, "The Myth of Posse Comitatus," *Journal of Homeland Security*, Homeland Security Institute, October 2000, available from *www.homelandsecurity.org/journal/articles/Trebilcock. htm#_edn1.*)

Under the Insurrection Act of 1807 (10 USC sections 331-335), when there are "insurrections in any State against its government," the President "may, upon the request of its legislature or of its governor . . . call into Federal service . . . the militia of the other States . . . and use such of the armed forces, as he considers necessary to suppress the insurrection." The Robert T. Stafford Disaster Relief and Emergency Assistance Act of 1988 (42 U.S.C. section 5121), authorizes the Federal government to help state and local governments alleviate the suffering and damage caused by disasters. The National Defense Authorization Act (NDAA) of 2007 considerably broadened Presidential authority to deploy troops within the United States. Under section 1042 of this act, the President could "deploy troops as a police force during a natural disaster, epidemic, serious public health emergency, terrorist attack, or other condition, when the President determines that the authorities of the state are incapable of maintaining public order." This occasioned a considerable backlash among the states, and was repealed by the subsequent 2008 NDAA. The Robert T. Stafford Disaster Relief and Emergency Assistance Act of 1988 (42 U.S.C. section 5121), authorizes the Federal government to help state and local governments alleviate the suffering and damage caused by disasters.

40. *Strategy for Homeland Defense and Civil Support*, Washington, DC: Department of Defense, The Pentagon, June 2005, p. 3. Dual capable forces are those with inherent capabilities that have application for both warfighting and civil support tasks. For example, DoD recognizes the value of these types of capabilities in relation to CBRNE response. The DoD Strategy for Homeland Defense and Civil Support states that,

> [w]ith the exception of a dedicated command and control element (currently the Joint Task Force-Civil Support) and the Army National Guard Weapons of Mass Destruction (WMD) Civil Support Teams, DoD will rely on dual-capable forces for the domestic consequence management [CM] mission. These dual-capable forces must be trained, equipped, and ready to provide timely assistance to civil authorities in times of domestic CBRNE catastrophes, programming for this capability when directed.

The DoD Joint Operating Concept for Homeland Defense and Civil Support states that:

> Warfighting forces with dual capability for CBRNE defense and domestic CBRNE CM operations must be identified,

trained, equipped, and exercised as necessary to assist civil authorities. This capability must include forces and assets able to provide agent detection and assessment, agent containment, quarantine, evacuation, force protection, decontamination, medical operations in a contaminated environment, and medical surge capabilities (including mortuary affairs).

Joint Operating Concept for Homeland Defense and Civil Support, Washington, DC: Department of Defense, The Pentagon, October 2007, p. 43. While the DoD discussion centers on CBRNE, there are obviously many other capabilities within our military forces which fall under the very broad characterization of dual capable, including medical, transportation, supply, air traffic control, and military police, to name but a few.

41. *National Guard Homeland Defense White Paper: September 11th, 2001, Hurricane Katrina and Beyond,* Arlington, VA: Chief, National Guard Bureau, pp. 6-8.

The command and control construct for the G8 Summit, DNC, RNC, and Operation Winter Freeze represent landmark achievements. For the first time in our nation's history, the National Guard attained unity of command for all military forces operating in support of a major event. In each case, from one Joint Force Headquarters, a single National Guard officer commanded Guard units from multiple States operating under Title 32 authority, as well as Active Component Army/Navy/Air Force/Marine Corps Title 10 forces in a joint, intergovernmental/interagency environment.

42. Ludwig J. Schumacher, "Dual Status Command for No-Notice Events: Integrating the Military Response to Domestic Disasters," *Homeland Security Affairs,* Vol. 7, Article 4, February 2011, pp. 4-5, available from *www.hsaj.org/?article=7.1.4.* In preparation for civil support operations in response to Hurricane Irene, DoD (for the first time) appointed four dual-status commanders from the North Carolina, New Hampshire, New York, and Rhode Island National Guards to "direct both federal active-duty forces and state National Guard forces," to "ensure that state and federal military forces . . . work effectively together," to prevent "duplication of effort, and provide the life-saving efforts that governors

request." "DoD Announces Hurricane Irene Dual-Status Commanders," News Release, Washington, DC: Office of the Assistant Secretary of Defense (Public Affairs), available from *www.defense.gov/Releases/Release.aspx?ReleaseID=14756.*

43. Department of Defense, Army Regulation 525-29, *Army Force Generation*, Washington, DC: U.S. Government Printing Office, December 14, 2010, p. 1.

44. John Jay, "The Same Subject Continued—Concerning the Dangers from Foreign Force and Influence," Clinton Rossiter, ed., *The Federalist Papers, No. 3*, New York: Signet Classic Edition, New American Library, 2003, p. 36.

U.S. ARMY WAR COLLEGE

Major General Gregg F. Martin
Commandant

*****

STRATEGIC STUDIES INSTITUTE

Director
Professor Douglas C. Lovelace, Jr.

Director of Research
Dr. Antulio J. Echevarria II

Authors
Lieutenant General (Retired) H Steven Blum
Lieutenant Colonel (Retired) Kerry McIntyre

Director of Publications
Dr. James G. Pierce

Publications Assistant
Ms. Rita A. Rummel

*****

Composition
Mrs. Jennifer E. Nevil